LOVE

IS AN EMOTION

THE BIBLE TELLS ME SO?

R. L. LEWIS

LUCIDBOOKS

Love Is an Emotion
The Bible Tells Me So?

Copyright © 2021 by R. L. Lewis

Published by Lucid Books in Houston, TX
www.lucidbookspublishing.com

Paperback ISBN: 978-1-63296-443-4
Hardback ISBN: 978-1-63296-450-2
eISBN: 978-1-63296-448-9

Special Sales: Most Lucid Books titles are available in special quantity discounts. Custom imprinting or excerpting can also be done to fit special needs. For standard bulk orders, go to www.lucidbooksbulk.com. For specialty press or large orders, contact Lucid Books at books@lucidbookspublishing.com.

For my wife, Kayla . . . obviously

TABLE OF CONTENTS

INTRODUCTION

Ask 10 different people to define the word *love*, and you might get 10 different definitions. Ask 10 different *Christians* to define love, and you might get more definitions than you can count. "Well, it depends on what kind of love you're talking about," one of them might say. "Are you talking about love for your neighbor? Love for your enemy? Love for your spouse? Love for your dog? Love for pizza? Love for sin? Love for God? God's love for you?" The answer can quickly become much more complicated than you ever imagined.

Nine times out of 10, however, you will find at least one common theme among all these answers: Whatever love is, it is *not* just an emotion. Most might even say that love is not an emotion at all—at least not Christian love.

But I disagree.

My perspective did not arise from some desire to be a contrarian—though I am hardly above such a temptation. Neither did my perspective arise from some inkling I had in the back of my mind all along—as if I always felt like love was an emotion but just lacked the words to competently prove it. In fact, in 2007, I remember sitting across the table from my mom trying to explain to her my confident conviction that God gave us emotions for one reason and one reason only: to say no to them. In my well-intentioned but misguided view, I believed that disregarding all emotion was actually an integral part of loving our neighbor as ourselves. And I suppose I was also on my way to becoming a Stoic monk tucked away in the mountains somewhere.

Nevertheless, I am of the generation that, for better or for worse, highly values sincerity. And while I faithfully employed the fake-it-'til-you-make-it mentality pervasive among many believers—sometimes, even wisely so—it eventually started to feel, well, fake. It was *practically* helpful in many ways, yes, but it didn't really seem like a sustainable approach to life. Nor did it provide an adequate explanation for why I even needed to fake it in the first place. My suspicion was on the rise.

Finally, a little more than a decade ago, amidst some of my toughest bouts with depression, I remember lying on the floor of my apartment in Chattanooga, Tennessee, and having a very disturbing thought. As I lay there in my distressed and dangerously irrational mental state, wondering how exactly Jesus might feel about me, this is what I falsely imagined him saying:

"To be honest, Rich, I don't really like you."

Wait. Come again?

"I mean, don't get me wrong. I still *love* you. And I'll still do everything I promised to do for you, but only because I have to—only because I said I would—not because I actually want to. Sure, I actually like doing those things for other believers. But for you? It's such a pain, especially since I feel absolutely nothing for you. But hey, love isn't about emotion. So don't worry about it. I don't have to like you. And, quite frankly, I don't."

Ouch! That really hurt.

Unfortunately, however, given my understanding of love as some sort of action or commitment, I had no reason to convince myself that these thoughts were altogether invalid. Sure, the image didn't feel quite right—and, of course, it wasn't. But since when does the fact that something doesn't feel quite right serve as proof of anything? Furthermore, didn't Jesus's alleged words to me reflect the very same thing I had told myself and others time and time again—that you don't have to *like* your neighbor, but you do have to *love* your neighbor? Or that real, Christian love isn't about desire but about duty? Why, then, couldn't those principles apply to Christ's love for me as well?

In truth, I was genuinely willing to accept the fact that the Lord simply felt no love for me. Even though the bleakness of that reality was not exactly comforting to my soul, I wasn't going to change my definition of love just to make me feel better about myself. After all, I would rather have truth inform my emotions than the other way around. But fortunately, instead of triggering even more depression within me, that experience on my apartment floor actually triggered my curiosity more than anything else, starting me on a journey that would lead me to a vastly different perspective.

Don't be alarmed, though. Despite the admittedly absurd, insecurity-based, depression-driven picture in my head that may have sparked my journey to better understand love, the line of reasoning I will present throughout this book proves to be far more objective in its content, which leads me to the following question: Why should you even listen to what I have to say?

I'll be honest, my educational background is in mathematics—not theology or psychology. I studied art for a few years, too, which probably doesn't help my credibility either. Still, with a background in mathematics, one of my self-proclaimed strengths rests in my ability to "show my work" as I carefully move toward a solution—a strength that would surely make my (very cool) high school math teachers proud. My goal, then, in this book is to guide you through a methodical progression of thought that allows you to evaluate the biblical data for yourself. And hopefully, I can do that concisely. I'm less interested in bombarding you with every possible argument and more interested in giving you a sufficient explanation you could swallow even in one sitting if you so dared.

Last, and oddly enough despite what the title of this book may suggest, my primary aim isn't to convince you that love is an emotion. No, my primary aim is to demonstrate how the view that love is an emotion—even if adopted only hypothetically for the sake of argument—can potentially strengthen our understanding of and deepen our appreciation for the glorious "gospel of the grace of God" (Acts 20:24). Thus, while the case for love's being an emotion is one I am eager to provide, the implications of love's being an emotion will turn out to be exceedingly more exciting—and challenging—to explore.

So let's get right into it.

Part 1

CANVASSING THE OPTIONS

Chapter 1

ACTION

In his letter to the Ephesians, Paul writes one of the most familiar and fundamental passages in all scripture. After reminding his readers that they were once dead in their sins and "were by nature children of wrath, like the rest of mankind" (Eph. 2:3), Paul continues:

> *But God, being rich in mercy, because of the great love with which he loved us, even when we were dead in our trespasses, made us alive together with Christ. . . . For by grace you have been saved through faith. And this is not your own doing; it is the gift of God, not a result of works, so that no one may boast.*
>
> —Eph. 2:4–5, 8–9

Notice what Paul highlights as one of the reasons behind this great act of redemption. The apostle states that God did so because of his great *love* for us. John also highlights an overarching motivation of love when he famously writes, "For God so loved the world, that he gave his only Son, that whoever believes in him should not perish but have eternal life" (John 3:16).

A reason for action is something altogether separate from the action itself. The reason motivates and consequently precedes the action in the same way a cause precedes its effect. Therefore, because God's love served as his reason for sending his Son to die for our sins, that love was and is something altogether distinct from his subsequent action.

"By this we know love," John explains to his readers, "that [Christ] laid down his life for us" (1 John 3:16). John also writes, "In this the love of God was made manifest among us, that God sent his only Son into the world, so that we might live through him" (1 John 4:9). As these passages plainly imply, we can come to know God's love only through his action to *show* us that love and make it manifest among us. Paul likewise evinces this principle when he states that "God *shows* his love for us in that while we were still sinners, Christ died for us" (Rom. 5:8, emphasis added).[1] However, this demonstration of love is

---

1. The author of Hebrews also uses this language when he commends his readers' love for the saints: "For God is not unjust so as to overlook your work and the love that you have *shown* for his name in serving the saints, as you still do" (Heb. 6:10, emphasis added). Their love was subsequently made known to others by their service.

not to be confused with the actual love that motivates and necessarily precedes it. For how can an action be motivated by love unless that love exists prior to that action?

Another way of expressing this distinction between love and action can be found in Paul's second letter to the Corinthians. Anticipating the arrival of Titus and two other church messengers, Paul writes, "So give proof before the churches of your love and of our boasting about you to these men" (2 Cor. 8:24). Paul already knew the Corinthians had such love; he simply wanted them to *prove* they had such love by their actions. We also must give proof of our love to others, just as Christ did when he "loved us *and* gave himself up for us" (Eph. 5:2, emphasis added). His death was the ultimate proof of his love. But this evidence of love is something distinctly separate from the actual love that compels it (i.e., the love that it subsequently serves to prove).

If we disregard this observation, however, and instead try to define love as the action it motivates or performs, then love cannot *be* something until it *does* something. But of course, love cannot *do* something unless it *is* something because love must first *be* something before it can then *do* something. Thus, love cannot logically be defined as what it does, and it must not be mistaken for whatever action it subsequently performs.

This same line of reasoning also discredits the idea that love might somehow still *include* action. For how can love paradoxically include something from which it is altogether separate? And how can its definition contain something that love is distinctly and thus definitively *not*?

Action without Love

Jesus tells his disciples that no one has a greater love than the person who "lay[s] down his life for his friends" (John 15:13). However, Paul builds an argument based in part on the notion that a person can "deliver up [his] body" and, hence, lay down his life without having any love at all (1 Cor. 13:3). In this particular case, then, the great love Jesus commends is found not in just any person who lays down his or her life but in those who specifically lay down their lives *for* their friends. An inward motivation can stand as the difference between two acts that outwardly look the same.

You'll find a similar instance of opposing motivations in Paul's letter to the Philippians. After noting how his imprisonment has emboldened many brothers "to speak the word without fear" (Phil. 1:14), Paul writes the following:

> *Some indeed preach Christ from envy and rivalry, but others from good will. The latter do it* out of love, *knowing that I am put here for the defense of the gospel. The former proclaim Christ* out of selfish ambition, *not sincerely*

but thinking to afflict me in my imprisonment
(emphasis added).

—Phil. 1:15–17

As the above passages show, neither the preaching of Christ nor the sacrificing of one's own life can sufficiently guarantee a motivation rooted in genuine love. Regardless of whether such love always implies action, action does not always imply love. In other words, no action is *necessarily* a loving action.

For an action to be done sincerely for others, something else must lie behind it that creates the difference between two acts that appear identical. That invisible *something*, known as love, motivates and separately precedes the action altogether.

Chapter 2

COMMITMENT

A truly loving person is undoubtedly committed to loving others. But whenever we commit to do something, we have not yet performed that action. Likewise, whenever we commit to love, we have not yet actually loved.

Of course, truly loving people do not stop at simply committing to love; they also go on to actually love. And they frequently do loving acts for others. So in order to avoid the paradoxical notion that a commitment to love is also love itself, perhaps we can, instead, try to define love as follows: Love is a commitment to actually do things for others.

However, a problem inevitably arises with this definition when we attempt to clarify what it means to do things *for* others.

According to the previous chapter, to do something sincerely for others means to do something out of genuine love. And according to our proposed definition of love, to do something out of genuine love means to do something out of a commitment to do things for others. Now, if we combine these two statements, we end up with the following definition: To do something *for* others means to do something out of a commitment to do things *for* others.

But that definition isn't helpful at all because it includes the very same words it is trying to define.

Here's the point. Any attempt to define love as some sort of decision or commitment to do something will always send us down a similarly circular trail of thought. Since no action is necessarily a loving action, the commitment to do a particular action—even if that action benefits someone else—does not imply that we are making that commitment out of love.[1] Some other motivation must still lie behind that commitment in order for it to be considered selfless and not just superficial. And, of course, that required motivation is love. Therefore, in the same way love cannot be defined as the action it subsequently performs, love also cannot be defined as the commitment it subsequently makes.

---

1. Even the act of committing itself (e.g., *to* someone) by nature of its still being an act may not necessarily be a loving act.

Still, I would like to point out that if you were to commit to do and then actually do to others "whatever you wish that others would do to you," you would, indeed, as Jesus explains, fulfill "the Law and the Prophets" (Matt. 7:12). This reality is not in question. But at this juncture, the focus is not on what it means to fulfill the law of God; rather, the focus is on what it means to love. And despite the unmistakable link between these two concepts, we cannot presuppose that their link implies their equivalence. Otherwise, we will foolishly begin this journey to understand what love is by operating under the assumption that we already know what love is.

Chapter 3

AGAPĒ

While speaking to his disciples in the upper room, Jesus says, "A new commandment I give to you, that you love one another: just as I have loved you, you also are to love one another" (John 13:34). The Greek word translated *love* in this passage is *agapaō*, which is the verb form of *agapē*. Jesus also uses this word when he responds to the Pharisees' question about "the great commandment in the Law" (Matt. 22:36):

> *You shall love the Lord your God with all your heart and with all your soul and with all your mind. This is the great and first commandment. And a second is like it: You*

shall love your neighbor as yourself. On these two commandments depend all the Law and the Prophets.

—Matt. 22:37–40

This word *agapē* is commonly used to represent a form of selfless, sacrificial love that believers willfully exercise regardless of how they feel. The primary aim of this perspective is to clarify how God could command us to love one another even though human emotions tend to fluctuate. However, a significant obstacle remains for those who hold to this common approach.

Even though the verb form of *agapē* is used in the previous commands to love God and one another, it also lies behind the following references:

- The tax collectors' and sinners' love for "those who love them" (Luke 6:32; Matt. 5:46)
- The Pharisees' love for the "best seat in the synagogues" (Luke 11:43)
- The nonbelievers' love for "the darkness rather than the light" (John 3:19)
- The authorities' love for the "the glory that comes from man" (John 12:43)
- Demas's love for "this present world" that caused him to desert Paul (2 Tim. 4:10)
- Balaam's love for the "gain from wrongdoing" (2 Pet. 2:15)

As evidenced by these examples, the understanding that *agapē* represents some sort of selfless love exercised by Christians unfortunately does not correspond with the word's collective use in scripture. On the contrary, all people, both believers *and* nonbelievers alike, possess the ability to express this form of love. Furthermore, such love can apparently be quite selfish and sinful at times. Why else would John exhort his readers to "not love [*agapaō*] the world or the things in the world" (1 John 2:15)?

Nevertheless, a distinction still remains between the love God commands and the love God condemns throughout the Bible. For instance, a couple of chapters after his exhortation not to love the world, John writes that "love is from God, and whoever loves has been born of God and knows God" (1 John 4:7). However, in light of his other statements referenced above, John cannot be implying that those who have not been born of God have no ability to love in general. Rather, in the context of his letter, John is referring to the love *for one another* motivated by the love God first "made manifest" through his Son (1 John 4:9). He clarifies this motivation even more plainly when he writes, "Beloved, if God so loved us, we also ought to love one another" (1 John 4:11).

"This is the message that you have heard from the beginning," John explains in an earlier chapter, "that we should love one another" (1 John 3:11). Jesus qualifies this love even more explicitly to his disciples when he states, "This is my commandment, that you love one another *as I have loved you*" (John 15:12, emphasis added). Such sacrificial love is obviously quite different from the love for the world that John denounces in his first letter (1 John 2:15). Yet this distinction lies not in some variable definition of love itself but in the contrast between each individual love's respective *object* and principal *motivation*.

When we love, we always love *something*. In God's commands throughout history, that something is specifically defined. For example, under the Mosaic Law, the Israelites were commanded to love God with all their being (Deut. 6:5) and to love their neighbors as themselves (Lev. 19:18). We, too, are commanded to love one another just "as Christ loved us and gave himself up for us" (Eph. 5:2). We are also commanded *not* to love certain things, especially those things that are evil (Rom. 12:9) and contrary to the truth (1 Cor. 13:6). In short, God calls us to have an *unselfish* love—a love that, conformed to Christ, seeks the benefit of others rather than ourselves. Such love, as we shall see in the next chapter, naturally fulfills every other command God has given us to follow as members of "the body of Christ" (1 Cor. 12:27). The distinct motivation behind such love will be examined more thoroughly in Part 3 of this book.

Varying Degrees

In addition to commanding us to love certain things, God also often specifies the degree to which we must love those things. For instance, you may love your neighbor to some extent, but God commands you to love your neighbor "as yourself" (Rom. 13:9; Gal. 5:14). Likewise, you may love God sincerely in your heart, but "the great and first commandment" of the Mosaic Law was to love him "with *all* your heart and with *all* your soul and with *all* your mind" (Matt. 22:37–38, emphasis added). Jesus even told his disciples that for them to be counted worthy of him, their love for him had to be so great that even their love for those closest to them paled in comparison (Matt. 10:37).

Keep in mind, however, that Jesus spoke this convicting conditional statement to his Jewish disciples under the law—not to the members of his body under grace. Though this distinction between law and grace will be addressed more fully in Part 4 of this book, I think that briefly acknowledging it here will help us keep Christ's words in their proper context.

As I hope to demonstrate in Chapter 7, none of us can actually be counted worthy of the Lord based on how much we love him or keep his commands. Why? Because no one actually loves or obeys God as abundantly and consistently as God's righteous standard demands. Nevertheless, I also hope to demonstrate in Chapter 7 that those who believe in "the gospel of the grace of

God" (Acts 20:24) are, in fact, counted worthy of the Lord by that glorious grace of God. They are justified in God's sight not because they have "a righteousness of [their] own that comes from the law" but because of the "righteousness from God" they have "through faith in Christ" and his saving work on the cross (Phil. 3:9).

Therefore, as we examine passages such as Matthew 10:37 that indirectly inform us about the Bible's treatment of the word *love*, we must be careful to view those passages in their appropriate biblical context. We must responsibly recognize their position in God's progressively revealed plan of redemption by considering not only what each passage says but also to whom each passage is directed.

Staying Consistent

As referenced in the first section of this chapter, Jesus himself tells us that "even sinners love [*agapaō*] those who love them" (Luke 6:32) and must, therefore, be capable of such *agapē* love. He doesn't delegitimize sinners' love for each other. He doesn't say, "But that isn't *real* love." No, nothing Jesus says implies anything other than the fact that sinners really do love those who love them. Of course, this observation doesn't mean that such love is pleasing to the Lord, for "without faith it is impossible to please him" (Heb. 11:6). Furthermore, the fact that they only love those who love them certainly suggests that their love has a selfishly conditional quality. Nevertheless, their love is *still* love.

Also, when John says that "people loved the darkness rather than the light because their works were evil" (John 3:19), he offers no indication that one kind of love loves the darkness and another kind of love loves the light. Instead, he allows the same concept of love to be applicable in either case. Therefore, we cannot somehow conclude that a love for the darkness is something a person, by definition, *feels* while a love for the light is something that a person, by definition, *chooses* regardless of how that person feels. No, in both cases, the general concept of love must stay consistent. Even though the outward *expression* of love may vary tremendously depending on the object and motivation of that love, the inherent *definition* of love remains unchanged.

Before continuing, I would like to note that through-out this book, I have only included New Testament references to love that contain the root word *agapē* or its verb form *agapaō*. I have chosen these for the sake of both brevity and consistency in order to guard against any accusation that my argument depends on a confusion of Greek terms. However, if you're interested in learning more about the proper distinction—or perhaps, at times, lack thereof—among the various Greek words translated *love* throughout the New Testament, I highly recommend Dr. Matthew A. Elliott's *Faithful Feelings: Rethinking Emotion in the New Testament.*

Chapter 4

OBEDIENCE

Just as a father who loves his son by no means fulfills his son's every request,[1] the fact that we love someone does not necessarily imply that we also obey that someone. Therefore, loving someone and obeying someone represent separate concepts that bear different meanings. Even though the two may exist simultaneously under certain circumstances, the presence of one does not guarantee the presence of the other. Otherwise, when Jesus says, "This is my commandment, that you love one another as I have loved you" (John 15:12), he would also be implying a second commandment to "obey one another as I have obeyed you." Such an inference would quite obviously be an absurd one to make.

---

1. In Proverbs 13:24, for example, a father who loves his son "is diligent to discipline him," even if that son desperately pleads otherwise.

Nevertheless, Jesus does say to his disciples, "If you love me, you will keep my commandments" (John 14:15). He also says, "If anyone loves me, he will keep my word" (John 14:23).[2] Thus, a love for the Lord actually *does* imply obedience to him. But if loving someone, in general, doesn't necessarily imply obedience to that someone, why does the fact that we love the Lord always imply that we will also obey him? Why can't we simply love him without obeying him?

Obviously, the answer cannot lie in the idea that loving God and obeying God represent two ways of saying the same thing. Again, a love for someone and obedience to that someone are two separate concepts that bear two different meanings. According to the previous chapter, the answer also cannot lie in some unique definition of *agapē*. Therefore, we are logically forced to conclude

---

2. Though this passage certainly helps further our understanding of how the Bible defines love, we must be careful to keep it in its proper context. To be clear, after Jesus says, "If anyone loves me, he will keep my word," he immediately adds, "and my Father will love him, and we will come to him and make our home with him" (John 14:23). Therefore, like the Matthew 10:37 passage I briefly addressed in Chapter 3, Jesus is again speaking to Jews under the law, not to the members of his body under grace. While the law may demand obedience in order to *gain* the Father's love, those under grace in Christ (i.e., those who are "in the Beloved" (Eph. 1:6)) already *have* the Father's love from which they can never be separated (Rom. 8:38–39). Through their faith in Christ and his saving work on the cross, they already have God's Spirit dwelling within them (e.g., 1 Cor. 3:16). Thus, while Jesus's statement in John 14:23 may demonstrate the fact that those who truly love him also always obey him, it does not yet reveal God's mystery of salvation for all who believe in the gospel of his grace.

that a love for God and obedience to God are indeed two distinct concepts. So the question still remains: Why can't we simply love God without obeying him?

In order to answer this question, we must first consider another curious association found in the Bible. In his letter to the Romans, Paul writes:

> *Owe no one anything, except to love each other, for the one who loves another has fulfilled the law. For the commandments, "You shall not commit adultery, You shall not murder, You shall not steal, You shall not covet," and any other commandment, are summed up in this word: "You shall love your neighbor as yourself."*
>
> —Rom. 13:8–9

Paul similarly tells the Galatians that "the whole law is fulfilled in one word: 'You shall love your neighbor as yourself'" (Gal. 5:14). Clearly, if we love our neighbor as ourselves, we will consequently fulfill every other command the Lord has given us. But if love and obedience are distinct concepts, what do the Lord's commands have to do with loving our neighbor?

Fortunately, at the same time Paul points out to the Romans that love is the fulfilling of the law, he also provides the reason why this observation about love must be true: "*Love does no wrong to a neighbor*; therefore love is the fulfilling of the law" (Rom. 13:10, emphasis added).

In other words, love's fulfillment of the law comes as a *result* or *consequence* of the fact that love does no wrong to a neighbor (i.e., the "wrong" as defined by scripture rather than by culture or personal opinion).

A result of an action is something that comes after the action itself. Therefore, in the same way that love cannot be defined as what it does, love also cannot be defined as the result of what it does. Otherwise, the result becomes the cause behind the action that then causes that result, a train of thought that makes no rational sense.

For instance, an Olympian does not win an event by first receiving a gold medal; the athlete receives a gold medal by first winning the event. The medal is what the Olympian collects as a result of the victory. Similarly, love does not "do no wrong to a neighbor" by first fulfilling the law; love inherently fulfills the law by simply doing no wrong to a neighbor.

Still, many people insist that Christian love is, by definition, obedience to God. In doing so, they unintentionally imply that the converse of Paul's statement is actually true: Love is the fulfilling of the law; therefore, love does no wrong to a neighbor. However, both Paul's statement and its converse cannot logically be true concurrently. The fact that love does no wrong to a neighbor cannot be the result of the fact that love is, by definition, obedience to the law. On the contrary, love fulfills the law by simply doing what it *naturally* does.

God's commands perfectly demonstrate what it means to do no wrong to a neighbor. They also outline the visible expression of what a perfect, selfless love for God and neighbor does by its very nature. Thus, John can say, "And this is love, that we walk according to [God's] commandments" (2 John 1:6; see also 1 John 5:3), because to walk *against* his commandments is equivalent to doing what such love never does. In fact, to walk against God's commandments is to show that you have no such love at all. However, this visible expression or demonstration of love must not be confused with the actual love that motivates it. In the same way that love cannot be defined as the inevitable action it performs, love also cannot be defined as the inevitable obedience in which it walks.

One and the Same

As we drill down more deeply into the logical implications, the connection between love and obedience can start to sound somewhat like a riddle. If love and obedience are different, what makes people who do them the same? Perhaps the following illustration will help show how this concept holds together.

Typically, in the middle of winter, people leave their lightweight jackets at home and instead wear their heaviest coats. However, if you happen to own only one jacket, then there is no distinction. The heaviest jacket you own is also the lightest jacket you own, and the lightest jacket is likewise the heaviest jacket.

Of course, the general concept of wearing your heaviest jacket is obviously still different from that of wearing your lightest jacket. Reducing the amount of clothing in your closet doesn't somehow invalidate this distinction. However, in your closet, you can choose only one jacket. Thus, you literally cannot wear your heaviest jacket without consequently wearing your lightest one as well.

The same conclusion is true regarding the person who loves God and the person who obeys God—there is no distinction between the two. The person who loves God is also the person who obeys God (see John 14:15, 23), and the person who obeys God is likewise the person who loves God (see John 14:21).

Of course, the general concept of loving someone is still different from that of obeying someone. Identifying God as the direct object of such love doesn't somehow invalidate this distinction. However, according to the Bible, people literally cannot love God as they ought (or their neighbor as themselves[3]) without consequently obeying God as well. In other words, the person who loves God and the person who obeys God are logically one and the same.

---

3. Recall that "the whole law is fulfilled in one word: 'You shall love your neighbor as yourself'" (Gal. 5:14).

Chapter 5

EMOTION

L uke recounts a story in which Jesus commends a
woman for the way "she loved much" (Luke 7:47).
In order to evidence the magnitude of her love,
Jesus says to his host, Simon:

> *Do you see this woman? I entered your house;*
> *you gave me no water for my feet, but she has*
> *wet my feet with her tears and wiped them with*
> *her hair. You gave me no kiss, but from the time*
> *I came in she has not ceased to kiss my feet. You*
> *did not anoint my head with oil, but she has*
> *anointed my feet with ointment.*
>
> —Luke 7:44–46

In light of the fact that love precedes action, we must consider what might lie behind this kissing, crying, and anointing that Jesus applauds. What could possibly cause a woman to wet the feet of Jesus with her tears and ceaselessly kiss them from the moment he entered Simon's house?

The answer is a simple one that represents what I humbly conceive to be the only explanation that can account for love's collective use in scripture.

Love is an emotion.

Of course, there are many objections that at first glance make this inductive argument's conclusion seem just as unreasonable as any other conclusion I've explored so far.

But consider the following questions:

- What other explanation could warrant the connotative contrast of love with an emotion like hate? (See Matt. 5:43, 6:24; Luke 16:13; John 12:25, 15:19; Rom. 9:13; Heb. 1:9; 1 John 4:20)
- What other explanation could fully illuminate the metaphorical sense of a love grown cold? (See Matt. 24:12)
- What other explanation could reasonably clarify what it means to "greet one another with the kiss of love"? (1 Pet. 5:14)
- What other explanation could effectively elucidate Paul's appeal for the Romans to "let love be genuine"? (Rom. 12:9; see also 2 Cor. 6:6)

- What other explanation could make sense of John's recurrent depiction of himself as "the disciple whom Jesus loved"? (John 21:20; see also John 13:23, 19:26, 21:7)

At the very least, doesn't the notion that love is an emotion make the above references so much simpler to comprehend? Consider also Mark's passing use of the word *love* when he records the conversation between Jesus and the rich young man: "And Jesus, looking at him, *loved* him, and said to him, 'You lack one thing: go, sell all that you have and give to the poor, and you will have treasure in heaven; and come, follow me'" (Mark 10:21, emphasis added). Is it not so much easier to understand that Mark is simply relaying the emotion Jesus felt for the man as he spoke with him?

Still, many questions could undoubtedly be asked to challenge this belief that love is an emotion—questions we'll explore in the chapters that follow.

Part 2

CONSIDERING
THE OBJECTIONS

Chapter 6

ACTION AND OBEDIENCE, REVISITED

In light of the proposition that love is an emotion, I want to emphasize the fact that obedience is obviously *not* an emotion. These separate concepts still bear different meanings. Nevertheless, those who truly love their neighbors as themselves clearly fulfill God's commands as a result, and to walk against his commands is simply to do what such love never does.

Therefore, while love may not be an action, a love *without* obedient action can hardly be labeled as the unselfish love God commands. Unless it is eventually expressed "in deed and in truth" (1 John 3:18), such love will remain invisible to everyone and prove beneficial to no one. After all, our love can only be made known to others by our deeds and actions just as God's love was made known to us by his action when he sent his Son to die for us on the cross (Rom. 5:8). In fact, even Christ's love for the Father was made known to us by his obedience, for he explains to his disciples, "I do as the Father has commanded me, so that the world may know that I love the Father" (John 14:31).

In the same way that we demonstrate the "work of faith" and the "steadfastness of hope in our Lord Jesus Christ," we also demonstrate the fruitful "labor of love" (1 Thess. 1:3) as we use our freedom in Christ to serve one another in light of our love and thus "*through* love" (Gal. 5:13, emphasis added). Consequently, whenever we don't use our freedom in this way, our actions can just as easily end up proving our *lack* of love.

For instance, while discussing the differences in conscience regarding unclean foods, Paul tells the Romans that "if your brother is grieved by what you eat, you are no longer walking in love" (Rom. 14:15). Here, Paul identifies an action—eating in a way that grieves a person's brother—that conclusively reveals a lack of love in the one who performs it. Why? Because "it is wrong for anyone to . . . do anything that causes [his] brother to stumble" (Rom. 14:20–21). Therefore, unselfish love would never do such a thing because "love does no wrong to a neighbor" (Rom. 13:10). Instead, such love compels us to "pursue what makes for peace and for mutual upbuilding" (Rom. 14:19). It compels us "not to please ourselves" but to "please [our] neighbor for his good" just as "Christ did not please himself" but chose to suffer for *our* good (Rom. 15:1–3).

The Bible is clear. Regardless of what emotion we might be feeling at the moment, any act in opposition to the Lord's commands is an act void of the love he commands us to have for one another. Hence, to say that love is an emotion is not to say that the love God commands is altogether subjective in its expression. Yes, love is something we feel, but God has no problem defining specific actions that those who genuinely love their neighbor as themselves will do. Consequently, every sin we commit testifies that we do not, in fact, love as we ought.

Nevertheless, while God's commands may indeed describe what unselfish love does, they do not serve as the means by which such love fulfills that description. In other words, we don't love our neighbor as ourselves *by* obeying God's commands. Instead, whenever we *do* truly love our neighbor as ourselves, we inevitably *will* obey God's commands. And the same is true of a genuine love for the Lord: "If you love me," Jesus says to his disciples, "you will keep my commandments" (John 14:15). If whatever love or emotion we are feeling causes us to do or even to desire to do something that opposes what God has called us to do, that emotion is contrary to the love God commands.

Burdensome Commands

Perhaps the understanding that love is an emotion can also help explain what John means when he states, "This is the love of God, that we keep his commandments. And his commandments are not burdensome" (1 John 5:3). How do we determine whether something is burdensome? Is it not through how we feel in the midst of that *something*? And if God's commands are the perfect expression of selfless love, what do they become when there is no love— no *emotion*—to be found? They become burdensome, indeed—like eating a food with a flavor you can't stand. You can physically eat it, yes, but the whole process will be detestable. Perhaps the same is true whenever we try to fulfill God's commands without the internal motivation they require. The consequent burden or aversion we feel stems from our lack of selfless love.

I do not mean to suggest, of course, that the Christian's life should be void of burden—such a statement would be both absurd and unbiblical for a myriad of reasons. At one point, even Paul and Timothy "were so utterly burdened beyond [their] strength that [they] despaired of life itself" (2 Cor. 1:8). No, the Christian's life may be filled with all kinds of burdens, struggles, and pain. Sometimes, those burdens (e.g., persecution) will even come as a direct result of keeping the Lord's commands. But for the one who loves the Lord above all else, the commands *themselves* are not burdensome—even if those commands end up leading to circumstances that certainly *are* burdensome.

Commitment, Revisited

Like the concept of obedience, marriage is also most certainly not an emotion. Instead, marriage is a type of commitment, and a commitment is an obligation we agree to fulfill regardless of how we feel. Marriage is a covenant, a relationship based on oath, not emotion. More importantly, marriage is a union in which a husband and a wife mysteriously "become one flesh" (Gen. 2:24). And even though it can find its initial motivation in love, marriage should never be confused or equated with the actual love itself. The commitment still remains even if the motivating emotion starts to wane, and so a loss of that emotion can never justify divorce.

However, if love itself is falsely perceived as a commitment, then we can potentially fulfill that commitment even when we feel no love at all. Consequently, in addition to *looking* like an act done out of legalism, moralism, or selfish ambition, an act of love can also *feel* like an act done out of legalism, moralism, or selfish ambition. Discerning the difference between the two becomes quite challenging if not impossible. However, love is not a commitment; love is an emotion. Hence, if we are acting out of love, we feel that love at least to some degree; if we aren't, we don't. Whether we feel it for our neighbor in the same way we feel it for ourselves, or whether we feel it *only* for ourselves with little concern for the good of our neighbor, one fact remains unchanged—love is, indeed, an emotion, and the person who has love can actually feel it.

So whenever we come across someone for whom we honestly feel no genuine love, we have a decision to make. Either we can redefine love to mean something that seems more manageable but ultimately proves illogical, or we can accept that love is an emotion and that if we don't feel it, we simply don't have it. I conceive that in addition to being far less complicated, only the latter represents the humbling truth.

Chapter 7

CAN GOD COMMAND EMOTION?

Whenever we experience an emotion, we genuinely feel it. Therefore, every time the Lord commands us to love, that love is something we are expected to *actually* feel—even when he commands us to love our enemies (see Matt. 5:44; Luke 6:27, 35). In other words, emotion is the obligation. To fulfill that obligation without that emotion is to fail at fulfilling that obligation altogether.

Obviously, no human being can simply conjure up a genuine emotion for someone else on command. This reality often serves as the primary reason to reject that love is an emotion. Unfortunately, this conclusion falsely assumes that the only way a person can fulfill a command to feel something is by conjuring up that emotion out of thin air. Yet even though God desires for us to feel the love he commands, he does not expect us to do so by willing such love into existence. The command isn't to *fabricate* love; the command is simply to *love*—a duty made feasible only through his Spirit (see Gal. 5:22).

More importantly, while our obedience to God requires our compliance with his commands, our amenability to his commands implies nothing about the *nature* of those commands. Obedience doesn't make the rules; it simply seeks to follow them. And it bears no implication that every command must reside within the boundaries of our human capacity or immediate volition. Because of this reality, I see no need to delineate an explanation for why God is "allowed" to command emotion, especially since his commands reflect *his* holiness and righteousness and goodness (see Rom. 7:12), not ours. Nevertheless, in Chapter 10, I will briefly elaborate on one potential theory that might help make such a command seem more reasonable from a philosophical perspective.

Finally, even if God's commands *do* appear to reside within the boundaries of our human capacity or immediate volition, Paul makes it clear that apart from Christ, no one has the ability to obey God by their own means. "For the mind that is set on the flesh is hostile to God, for it does not submit to God's law; indeed, it *cannot*. Those who are in the flesh *cannot* please God" (Rom. 8:7–8, emphasis added).

The Gospel of God's Grace

Our inability to fully fulfill God's commands helps clarify why "all who rely on works of the law" in order to be justified—or declared righteous—before God "are under a curse; for it is written, 'Cursed be everyone who does not abide by *all* things written in the Book of the Law, and do them'" (Gal. 3:10, emphasis added). Of course, no one *can* do them all. Thus, "by works of the law no human being will be justified in [God's] sight, since through the law comes knowledge of sin" (Rom. 3:20).

Even those of us who were never under the Mosaic Law in the first place—a law given specifically to the Israelites under the Old Covenant—are still without excuse. Paul makes this reality clear when he writes the following:

> *For when Gentiles, who do not have the law, by nature do what the law requires, they are a law to themselves, even though they do not have the law. They show that the work of the law is written on their hearts, while their conscience also bears witness, and their conflicting thoughts accuse or even excuse them on that day when, according to my gospel, God judges the secrets of men by Christ Jesus.*
>
> —Rom. 2:14–16

Just as those "who have sinned under the law will be judged by the law," those "who have sinned without the law will also perish without the law" (Rom. 2:12). In either case, Paul assures us that "none is righteous, no, not one," for "all, both Jews and Greeks, are under sin" (Rom. 3:9–10). As inherently corrupt descendants of Adam—the man whose "one trespass led to condemnation for all men" (Rom. 5:18)—we all stand guilty before God, whose righteous standard demands nothing less than perfection. None of us "will be justified in [God's] sight" by our own works (Rom. 3:20) because no human being apart from Christ is without sin. Hence, we all deserve nothing but "wrath and fury" in God's impartial judgment to come (see Rom. 2:5–11).

"But now the righteousness of God has been manifested apart from the law," that is, "the righteousness of God through faith in Jesus Christ for all who believe" (Rom. 3:21–22). Paul continues:

> For there is no distinction: for all have sinned and fall short of the glory of God, and are justified by his grace as a gift, through the redemption that is in Christ Jesus, whom God put forward as a propitiation by his blood, to be received by faith.
>
> —Rom. 3:22–25

This "faith comes from hearing, and hearing through the word of Christ" (Rom. 10:17). Regardless of age or perceived cognitive ability, those who hear and thereupon believe are "justified by faith *apart* from works of the law" (Rom. 3:28, emphasis added).

According to the now disclosed "mystery of the gospel" (Eph. 6:19) that God had formerly "kept secret for long ages" (Rom. 16:25), God provided a means of salvation through which he could be both "just and the justifier of the one who has faith in Jesus" (Rom. 3:26). He sent his sinless Son, Jesus Christ, who was both fully God and fully man (see Rom. 1:3–4), to "[die] for our sins" and then be "raised on the third day" (1 Cor. 15:3–4) so we could be "justified by his blood" and consequently "saved by him from the wrath of God" to come (Rom. 5:9). The fact that Christ's sacrifice was a *propitiation* for our sins (see Rom. 3:25) means he wholly satisfied God's righteous wrath against us by paying the penalty for those sins in full. Now, through our faith in that payment, we are completely "reconciled to God" (Rom. 5:10) and given the sure "hope of eternal life" in Christ (Titus 1:2).

Though Jesus "knew no sin," God "made him to be sin" for us "so that in him we might become the righteousness of God" (2 Cor. 5:21). In other words, God imputed our sins to Christ on the cross as if they were his own so that (1) Christ could legitimately die for those sins in our place, and (2) God could graciously impute Christ's righteousness to us through faith (i.e., credit his perfect righteousness to our account as a gift).

What a magnificent deal for us! And what a magnanimous sacrifice on the part of Christ! He "redeemed us from the curse of the law" we were under because of our sin "by becoming a curse for us" on the cross so that, in him, we could receive "the blessing of Abraham" (Gal. 3:13–14)—justification by faith *apart* from works of the law (Gal. 3:5–9; see also Rom. 4). So those who trust not in their own works but in the risen Christ's saving work on their behalf are thereafter forgiven of their sins and declared righteous in God's sight by grace. "There is therefore now no condemnation" left for them to bear (Rom. 8:1).

Still, even when we come to believe this glorious gospel of grace, God does not expect us to conjure up genuine emotion out of thin air. Again, the impossible task of fabricating love is not at all what God commands of us. However, whenever we inevitably lack genuine love for him or one another, God *does* command us to *pursue* such love even as we wholly depend on his Spirit to produce that love—a pursuit I will address in Chapter 13.

Chapter 8

SUBJECTIVITY AND SACRIFICE

One of the greatest forms of resistance to the claim that love is an emotion stems from the inherent relationship between emotion and subjectivity. Some fear that if they agree love is an emotion, the Christian life will somehow morph into this indefinable blob of subjective experience and sentimentalism. However, like the fear regarding emotion and its impact on marriage, this concern is fortunately also an unfounded one.

First, the belief that love is something we feel does not somehow negate the fact that scripture is authoritative in our lives. Second, regardless of whatever emotion we might be feeling at the moment, any act (or word, thought, or

desire) that opposes the Lord's commands is an act completely void of the love he commands us to have for one
another. Thus, the "rightly [handled] . . . word of truth"
(2 Tim. 2:15) remains the foremost standard by which we
evaluate the fruit of whatever love we profess to feel.

For instance, if you claim to love me as yourself but
then turn around and steal from me when I'm not looking,
the Bible allows me to objectively conclude you do not
love me as yourself (see Rom. 13:9). And this conclusion
has absolutely nothing to do with what you might have
been feeling at the time.

For another more personal example, suppose I grow
impatient or irritable with my wife one morning. Though I
do genuinely love my wife, I can objectively conclude that
I do not, in fact, love her to the same extent that "Christ
loved the church and gave himself up for her" (Eph.
5:25). I can objectively conclude that I do not love her *as
myself*—at least not in the perfect way to which I aspire.
Why? Because Paul writes that such love "is patient"
(1 Cor. 13:4), and in that moment, I most certainly was
not. He also writes that such love "is not irritable" (1 Cor.
13:5), and in that moment, I most certainly was.[1] And
even though this example may initially offend some, this
offense lies at the heart of why it's so important for us to

---

1. Fortunately, my gracious wife was never under the impression that she
was marrying a perfect man. Still, I pray my love for her will grow more
and more like Christ's each day.

understand that love is an emotion. Otherwise, we will end up downplaying the true standard of God's perfect righteousness.

Context and Equivocation

Even when we sincerely *do* feel motivated by love, we are not thereby vindicated in whatever action we take. Why? Because according to Part 1 of this book, love *itself* can be sinful under certain circumstances. For instance, a man might argue, "I'm only sleeping with my girlfriend because I love her." And his claim might legitimately be true in the general, unqualified sense of the word *love*. I have no theological reason or need to engage in some subjective argument otherwise. However, according to the Bible, the specific love God commands us to have for one another always results in obedience to him. Consequently, whenever a man participates in any kind of sexual activity with any individual who is not currently his wife, he clearly does not love that individual in the same selfless way that God commands him to love. And he certainly does not love God above all else because he is directly opposing God's command to abstain from such sexual immorality. The sinfulness of his behavior exposes the sinfulness of his love. No amount of sincere emotion can change that reality.

Still, some may dispute, "As long as I am acting out of genuine love, what's the problem? Isn't that what God wants me to do? And doesn't the Bible say that God *is* love?" Whether or not they realize their error, those who appeal to love in order to justify their sinful behavior are committing the fallacy of equivocation. In other words, they are ambiguously using the word *love* in two different ways within the same line of reasoning. Thus, their seemingly coherent argument is based on a misleading use of language.

However, the love God commands us to have for one another never leads to an action disobedient to any other command. Therefore, any love that *does* lead to a sinful, disobedient action is not the love God commands but the love God condemns. In light of this critical distinction, whenever we cite that "God is love" (1 John 4:8) or that he most certainly wants us to love one another (see Rom. 13:8), we must be careful not to strip the word *love* from its proper biblical context.

Laying Down One's Life

One of the hallmark traits of unselfish love Paul highlights is that "it does not insist on its own way" (1 Cor. 13:5). Instead, unselfish love compels us to "look not only to [our] own interests, but also to the interests of others" (Phil. 2:4). Unselfish love compels us not to "seek [our] own good, but the good of [our] neighbor" (1 Cor. 10:24). This compulsion clarifies why those who love their neighbor as themselves might feel like doing one thing but choose to do something else for the sake of their neighbor—even if that something else isn't very pleasant at all. And, of course, we find no greater example of this than in the willing sacrifice of Jesus on the cross.

Shortly before his arrest in the garden of Gethsemane, Jesus told Peter, James, and John, "My soul is very sorrowful, even to death" (Matt. 26:38; Mark 14:34). He then went away three times and prayed, "My Father, if it be possible, let this cup pass from me" (Matt. 26:39; see also Mark 14:36; Luke 22:42). His goal, after all, was not merely suffering for the sake of suffering. At the end of each prayer, however, he always made his foremost desire clear by saying, "Nevertheless, not as I will, but as you will" (Matt. 26:39). Though Jesus honestly wanted to avoid the suffering before him if possible, he most certainly wanted to accomplish the work of his Father infinitely more. No task was more important to him because that is what he "[came] down from heaven" to do (John 6:38; see also John 4:34).

During his earlier discourse to the disciples, Jesus said, "Greater love has no one than this, that someone lay down his life for his friends" (John 15:13). But Christ's love proved even greater in its depth because he "died for us" even "while we were still sinners" (Rom. 5:8). He showed his immeasurably great love for us—His great *emotion* for *you* and for *me*—by voluntarily laying down his life to save us from the power and penalty of sin. Through him, we who once were under God's righteous wrath now "have peace with God" by grace "since we have been justified by faith" (Rom. 5:1). And rather than deciding against *all* emotion, I contend that our Lord Jesus Christ was selflessly motivated by his *deepest* emotion—his great love for both the Father and for humankind.

Part 3

CONFIRMING THE FOUNDATION

Chapter 9

THE REASON BEHIND
OUR LOVE

After Simon belittled the sinful woman crying at Jesus's feet, Jesus told the following story: "A certain moneylender had two debtors. One owed five hundred denarii, and the other fifty. When they could not pay, he cancelled the debt of both. Now which of them will love him more?" (Luke 7:41–42).

From this story, Jesus expected Simon to have all the information he needed to answer the question correctly. And, of course, he *did* answer correctly: "The one, I suppose, for whom he cancelled the larger debt" (Luke 7:43). He gave a simple answer based on a logical thought process that Jesus affirmed as the *right* thought process: "You have judged rightly" (Luke 7:43).

Notice that Jesus did not ask Simon whether the debtors *would* love the moneylender. He already assumed they would. And Simon did not disagree. Why? Because the debtors obviously had a *reason* to love the moneylender. Thus, in addition to having an object, love also had a reason that motivated it. Even God's love for his Son affirms this principle: "For this reason the Father loves me, because I lay down my life that I may take it up again" (John 10:17).

Both debtors legitimately loved the moneylender because both had been forgiven. But one of them loved the moneylender more because his reason for loving him was obviously greater; his debt had been much larger than the other person's. Hence, the greater reason produced the greater love. And more specifically in this case, the greater forgiveness produced the greater love.

Still, regardless of the amount owed, neither debtor could actually pay back his debt. The same is true for Simon, but unlike the second debtor in Jesus's parable, Simon's need for forgiveness is not any less severe than the woman's need. He simply can't see it. Indeed, we all desperately need forgiveness because "all have sinned and fall short of the glory of God" (Rom. 3:23). None of us can pay back the debt of our sin. But when we recognize this condemning debt and, like the woman in this story,[1] come to

---

1. When Jesus says that "her sins, which are many, are forgiven—for she loved much" (Luke 7:47), he is not saying she was forgiven *because* she

believe in the great forgiveness (and righteousness[2]) found in Christ, we cannot help but love him. In fact, we cannot help but love one another as a result as well.

Love and Lovability

The Bible does not incite us to love one another by introducing some new kind of love believers must willfully exercise rather than genuinely feel. Instead, the Bible speaks of a merciful God who loved us so much that he "did not spare his own Son but gave him up for us all" (Rom. 8:32). Paul also writes:

> For while we were still weak, at the right time
> Christ died for the ungodly. For one will scarcely
> die for a righteous person—though perhaps for

---

loved much. That conclusion would contradict the parable he just told, for the two debtors' love was clearly a *result* of and a *response* to their forgiveness. Furthermore, in the same way that, as Jesus explains in the next sentence, "he who is forgiven little, loves little" (Luke 7:47), he who is forgiven much subsequently loves much as well. Therefore, the converse conclusion must be true for the woman in this story; she loved so much because she had been forgiven so much. Jesus is simply explaining to those around him that they could tell that her many sins had already been forgiven because of the way she loved him so much.

2. Unlike the woman in this story, we know of something far more glorious than what she could ever have imagined at that time. We believe in the later revealed gospel of God's grace that proclaims Christ's death for our sins and resurrection for our justification (see 1 Cor. 15:1–4; Rom. 4:25). And we understand that through our faith in him and his saving work on the cross, we are not only forgiven for our sins but also declared righteous in God's sight by grace.

a good person one would dare even to die—but God shows his love for us in that while we were still sinners, Christ died for us.

—Rom. 5:6–8

Our growing understanding of this great love revealed in the gospel consequently causes what was formerly unlovable to actually and sincerely become lovable in our eyes. Why? Because according to Paul's statement above, we are all the ungodly, unlovable ones whom God *did* love enough to give up his only Son. We are all the formerly condemned ones who "have now been justified by [Christ's] blood" through faith (Rom. 5:9). And if God so loved us, how can we not love one another as a result? Yes, we owe[3] even our enemies the same love Christ first showed us, for even "while *we* were enemies we were reconciled to God by the death of his Son" (Rom. 5:10, emphasis added).

But notice the distinction. Our view of *love* does not change in order to apply to those for whom we feel no love; rather, our view of what is *lovable* changes through the knowledge of him who saved us by grace through faith. His "great love with which he loved us" (Eph. 2:4) grants us a new perspective that subsequently changes the things our hearts are drawn to love. This gradual

---

3. Paul uses this language of *owing* love when he writes, "Owe no one anything, except to love each other, for the one who loves another has fulfilled the law" (Rom. 13:8).

transformation comes "by the renewal of [our] mind[s]" (Rom. 12:2) as we imbibe the truth of God's Word and let it shape the way we think, feel, and behave.

Consider, for example, the reason to which Paul attributes the Colossians' love for one another.

> *We always thank God, the Father of our Lord Jesus Christ, when we pray for you, since we heard of your faith in Christ Jesus and of the love that you have for all the saints,* because of the hope laid up for you in heaven. *Of this you have heard before in* the word of the truth, the gospel (emphasis added).
>
> —Col. 1:3–5

Also notice what he writes to Timothy regarding such love.

> *As I urged you when I was going to Macedonia, remain at Ephesus so that you may charge certain persons not to teach any different doctrine, nor to devote themselves to myths and endless genealogies, which promote speculations rather than the stewardship from God that is by faith. The aim of our charge is* love that issues from a pure heart and a good conscience and a sincere faith (emphasis added).
>
> —1 Tim. 1:3–5

That faith is, of course, in "Christ Jesus our Lord" (1 Tim. 1:2), who "came into the world to save sinners" (1 Tim. 1:15) and "gave himself as a ransom for all" (1 Tim. 2:6).

Even when Paul writes to the Ephesians about loving one another, he does so by directing their attention back to Christ. Instead of simply telling them they need to walk in love, he urges them to "walk in love, *as Christ loved us and gave himself up for us*, a fragrant offering and sacrifice to God" (Eph. 5:2, emphasis added).

In each of these passages, Paul demonstrates how closely connected our love for one another is to our deepening faith in Christ and the love he first showed for us on the cross. The fact that he died for us even though we were sinners lacking any kind of reciprocal love for him now stands as the motivation behind our love for others. *He* is the enduring foundation from which all God-honoring love flows. As we grow in our knowledge of him and let his Word "dwell in [us] richly" (Col. 3:16), our love for both God and our neighbor will naturally grow by the Spirit as well. This reality demonstrates in part why Paul prays for the Philippians' love to:

> *Abound more and more, with* knowledge *and all discernment, so that you may approve what is excellent, and so be pure and blameless for the day of Christ, filled with the fruit of righ-*

teousness that comes through Jesus Christ, to
the glory and praise of God (emphasis added).

—Phil. 1:9–11

Of course, because of the sinful flesh still present within us, we will regularly fail to love one another as Christ so selflessly loved us. But whatever unselfish love we *do* end up having will come only as a response to the great love God revealed through the cross.

Unconditional Love

Before I move on to the next chapter, I'd like to note that love's having a reason does not mean love can never be unconditional. On the contrary, love proves unconditional if there are no conditions under which its reason will change. For instance, suppose a mother loves her child simply because he is her child. That child can do nothing to change her love for him. Why? Because regardless of what he does, he will always be her child. And that is the primary reason she loves him in the first place. Such love can be considered a deep love because its reason is rooted in an immutable reality.

Now, suppose a man loves a woman simply because she is physically attractive to him. When she no longer proves attractive to him, he will no longer love her. Such love can be considered a shallow love because its reason is rooted in a fleeting condition.

In these two scenarios, both the deep, selfless love of the mother for her son and the shallow, selfish love of the man have a reason. However, only the selfless love proves unconditional because under no conditions will its reason ever change. Its condition, in a sense, has already been permanently met. No matter what the son does, he will never lose his status as his mother's child. With this picture in mind, what great comfort we should find in knowing that we who believe in Christ have been adopted as *God's* children. Yes, "the Spirit himself bears witness with our spirit that we are children of God" and "fellow heirs with Christ" (Rom. 8:16–17).

Chapter 10

A COGNITIVE VIEW OF EMOTION

Some scholars appeal to a cognitive theory of emotion to help explain why we can be held responsible for what we feel. Though varying perspectives exist within this cognitive approach to emotion, they all essentially assert that our emotions are produced by our cognitions (i.e., our thoughts, evaluations, and beliefs).[1] This stance may also help clarify the prior chapter's claim that our love always has a reason behind it—even if that reason lies beyond our conscious mind.[2]

---

1. Matthew A. Elliott, *Faithful Feelings: Rethinking Emotion in the New Testament* (Grand Rapids, MI: Kregel Publications, 2006), 31–32.
2. Elliott, *Faithful Feelings*, 42.

In the previously mentioned book *Faithful Feelings*, Dr. Matthew A. Elliott writes, "We are responsible for our emotions because they are based on beliefs and evaluations. They provide us with a picture of our true values."[3] Therefore, "when the New Testament commands emotion," Elliott argues, "it is exhorting the believer to have the values and beliefs out of which godly emotions flow,"[4] including unselfish love.[5] And we, of course, are responsible for whatever values and beliefs we hold.

What then becomes the point of even commanding emotion? Why not simply command us to believe and value the right things? Elliott proposes the following:

> In commanding the emotion, the writer puts their finger on the true indicator of *whether* these beliefs and values are *genuinely* held by the believer. There can be no self-deception or hiding behind simple intellectual assent when emotions are commanded.[6]

---

3. Elliott, 39.

4. Elliott, 143.

5. In keeping with his cognitive view of emotion, Elliott defines love as "an attraction towards an object" that "is the result of seeing a quality in [that] object that is good, valuable, or desirable. This definition," he argues, "is the only definition which will allow love to function as the root of all other emotions" (*Faithful Feelings*, 135).

6. Elliott, 144.

Perhaps Elliott's perspective helps explain why Paul mentions "those who are perishing, because they refused to love the truth and so be saved" (2 Thess. 2:10). Since the Bible clearly states that those who *believe* in the truth will be saved (see 2 Thess. 2:13), what could Paul possibly mean? Ultimately, these people will indeed "be condemned" because they "did not *believe* the truth but had pleasure in unrighteousness" (2 Thess. 2:12, emphasis added). But the truth of the gospel through which God calls us to be saved (see 2 Thess. 2:13–14) is quite literally *good news* to those who honestly believe it. And the only person who doesn't love good news is the one who doesn't believe it's good news in the first place. So perhaps this connection between a genuine belief in the truth and a resulting love for the truth is so inevitable in the context of the gospel of grace that Paul has no problem using the two interchangeably, at least this once.

The Need for Change

In Elliott's second book, *Feel: The Power of Listening to Your Heart*, he explains, "We often make the mistake of saying our emotions are wrong, when much of the time they're perfectly right—just based on the wrong information."[7] Thus, if we want to change our emotion, we can theoretically do so not "by dwelling on the

---

7. Matthew A. Elliott, *Feel: The Power of Listening to Your Heart* (Carol Stream, IL: Tyndale House Publishers, 2008), 145.

emotion itself" but "by dwelling on and changing the beliefs and evaluations that lie behind it."[8]

For example, if you believe butterflies sting like bees, you have a perfectly logical reason to feel afraid whenever you see a butterfly flying toward you. Nevertheless, this reason that drives your quite rational fear is unfortunately based on a wrong understanding and belief about butterflies. This fear will never cease to be until your understanding genuinely changes, but hopefully you can eventually come to enjoy the presence of a butterfly without being scared of its supposed sting.

However, even if a cognitive view of emotion *does* prove true to a certain extent, the sinful nature we inherited from Adam still leaves us a with a seemingly incurable problem. While our sinful emotions may be based on *wrong* information, our unregenerate minds remain impervious to the *right* information found in God's Word. As Paul writes in his first letter to the Corinthians, "the natural person does not accept the things of the Spirit of God, for they are folly to him,

---

8. Elliott, *Faithful Feelings*, 38. Note, however, that Elliott considers "it . . . also critical that we do not understand a cognitive view of emotions as a simple approach to the study of emotions. Emotions are highly complex phenomena that rely upon both our conscious and unconscious mind, memories, cultural factors, family upbringing, and our personalities. These factors interact and respond to one another in an incredibly complex web of interdependent beliefs and values to produce particular emotions in particular circumstances" (42).

and he is not able to understand them because they are spiritually discerned" (1 Cor. 2:14). He must first receive "the Spirit who is from God" before he can ever "understand the things freely given us by God" (1 Cor. 2:12). And without that Spirit, he most certainly cannot bear the "fruit of the Spirit" (Gal. 5:22), including the love God commands. Therefore, we must recognize that a believer's love for God and neighbor is not *just* a cognitive response to the fact that God loved us and sent his Son to die for us. It is also primarily the result of a change God must first work in us by his Spirit—a change we are powerless to elicit through our own efforts.

God not only grants us a new motivation for unselfish love; he also regenerates and renews us (see Titus 3:5) and, in so doing, makes us *capable* of having such unselfish love by his Spirit. Indeed, those who believe Christ "was delivered up for our trespasses and raised for our justification" (Rom. 4:25) are "set free from sin" and made "alive to God in Christ Jesus" (Rom. 6:7, 11). They are "sealed with the promised Holy Spirit" (Eph. 1:13) by whom they can now be taught the "spiritual truths" of God's Word (1 Cor. 2:13). And as the "new self" they have put on in Christ "is being renewed in knowledge after the image of its creator" (Col. 3:10), this "spiritually discerned" knowledge of God (1 Cor. 2:14) begins to naturally produce a great love within them.

A Spiritual Reaction

Perhaps the impact the knowledge of God has on our hearts is somewhat like taking a cup of vinegar and pouring a little baking soda into it. The combination of the two sparks a chemical reaction that produces carbon dioxide, and the solution immediately starts to bubble. We are not in control of this reaction; it simply happens naturally after the two substances are combined.

In the same way, as we grow in our understanding of "the things of the Spirit of God" (1 Cor. 2:14), that deepening knowledge rooted in faith sparks an internal reaction that produces a love we sincerely feel for both God and one another. We are not in conscious control of this reaction; it simply happens naturally as we mature through an increasing knowledge of God and his will.

Unfortunately, however, because of our sinful flesh, the impact that the things of God have on our hearts is actually more like taking a cup of *water* and pouring a little baking soda into it. The combination of the two doesn't spark anything at all. And unless that water is somehow changed into vinegar, no carbon dioxide bubbles will ever be produced.

We, then, are like that water, having absolutely no ability to positively react to or even understand the things of God unless we first receive his Spirit by trusting in the gospel of his Son. *God* is the one who must regenerate and renew us (see Titus 3:5). *God* is the one who alone can bring us "from death to life" in Christ (Rom. 6:13). We are simply the water, sitting utterly powerless to transform on its own.

Still, even this modified version of our overly simplistic metaphor fails to account for the subsequent battle to "walk by the Spirit" in order "not [to] gratify the desires of the flesh" (Gal. 5:16). Those who, by faith, already "*have* put on the new self" in Christ (Col. 3:10, emphasis added) are nevertheless charged "*to* put on the new self" in their daily lives (Eph. 4:24, emphasis added) because they regularly face the temptation to walk in their "former manner of life" instead (Eph. 4:22). But the cardinal point of the metaphor remains—apart from Christ and his Spirit working within us, we simply cannot walk in the selfless love he first showed us on the cross. Only he can "make [us] increase and abound in love for one another and for all" (1 Thess. 3:12).

Therefore, the claim that love is an emotion produced by an intricate complex of cognitions does not contradict the certain reality that our unselfish love is still a fruit *of the Spirit*. After all, the ability to understand or explain a process is something entirely different from the ability to actually cause that process to occur. Just as farmers who plant and water their seeds ultimately depend on God to "[give] the growth"

(1 Cor. 3:7), we can cultivate[9] the love that comes by the renewal of our minds (see Rom. 12:2) even as we credit the resulting transformation to the Spirit.

This reality demonstrates why many people can and do live lives filled with immense love for both God and their neighbors even though they may not agree that love is an emotion. Ultimately, such love grows out of a humble faith in and an increasing knowledge of Christ—not out of the understanding that love is an emotion. All believers "have been taught by God to love one another" in light of his grace (1 Thess. 4:9). And all believers are promised that if they walk by the Spirit, he will bear such fruit within them (see Gal. 5:16, 22).

Furthermore, the fact that a person agrees that love is an emotion by no means implies that this person will love their neighbor sincerely. I can certainly testify to this unfortunate reality. No, regardless of which view a person holds, we all sin and fall incomprehensibly short of the love God commands. Yet despite the deficiency of our love, God's love for us in Christ never ends, and he has forever proven that love by sending his Son to die for our sins.

---

9. The author of Hebrews encourages his readers to "consider how to stir up one another to love and good works" (Heb. 10:24). We, too, can help each other grow in unselfish love as we teach, admonish, encourage, and pray for one another in light of God's Word (see Col. 3:16). Nevertheless, we attribute the increase of our love not to ourselves but to the Lord (1 Thess. 3:12).

Part 4
CLARIFYING THE IMPLICATIONS

Chapter 11

NOW WHAT?

What exactly are we supposed to do when we don't love someone as we ought? One potentially frustrating fact about the command to love one another is that it doesn't actually tell us what to do. It only tells us what to feel. The command itself doesn't tell us *how* to feel it, and it certainly doesn't give us the *ability* to feel it; it simply tells us that we *should* feel it. And if we don't, then we are breaking that command.

So no, the command itself isn't telling us, for instance, to simply do whatever we feel like doing. Such wisdom proves unsound for both believer and nonbeliever alike. After all, even though we who belong to Christ have his Spirit dwelling within us (see Rom. 8:9), many of the desires we end up feeling in this life will stem from the flesh, not the Spirit. Unfortunately, "the desires of the flesh are against the Spirit" just as "the desires of the Spirit are against the flesh, for these are opposed to each other, to keep you from doing the things you want to do" (Gal. 5:16–17).

While the passions of the flesh can often feel so good and so right in the moment, they are nevertheless based on the darkened understanding we once had apart from Christ (see Eph. 4:18). They are part of the "old self, which belongs to [our] former manner of life and is corrupt through deceitful desires" (Eph. 4:22). However, the apostle Paul assures those of us who believe in his gospel[1] that "our old self was crucified with [Christ] in order that the body of sin might be brought to nothing, so that we would no longer be enslaved to sin. For one who has died has been set free from sin" (Rom. 6:6–7). Consequently, as we look not to our emotions but to the cross, we "must

---

1. To highlight "the stewardship of God's grace that was given to [him] for [us]," and to emphasize, for example, "how the mystery [of Christ] was made known to [him] by revelation" but "was not made known to the sons of men in other generations" (Eph. 3:1–5), Paul calls the gospel of God's grace *his* gospel three times (see Rom. 2:16, 16:25; 2 Tim. 2:8). This is the "gospel of God" for which he was "set apart" (Rom. 1:1)—the gospel he received "not . . . from any man" but "through a revelation of Jesus Christ" (Gal. 1:12). Thus, when Paul explains "[his] gospel and the preaching of Jesus Christ," he does so "according to the revelation of the mystery that was kept secret for long ages but has now been disclosed" (Rom. 16:25–26). He preaches Christ's death *for our sins* and triumphant resurrection on the third day (see 1 Cor. 15:1–4).

consider [ourselves] dead to sin and alive to God in Christ Jesus" (Rom. 6:11) because we really *are* dead to sin and alive to God in Christ Jesus. Our old self was crucified with Christ; we are no longer enslaved to sin. And we can confidently believe this truth about ourselves because God has clearly revealed it to us in the scriptures.

> *Let not sin therefore reign in your mortal body, to make you obey its passions. Do not present your members to sin as instruments for unrighteousness, but present yourselves to God as those who have been brought from death to life, and your members to God as instruments for righteousness. For sin will have no dominion over you, since you are not under law but under grace.*
>
> —Rom. 6:12–14

Rather than granting us the freedom *to* sin, being under God's grace actually implies that we have "been set free *from* sin" (Rom. 6:7, emphasis added) so that we can live in service to God and walk in righteousness. This saving "grace in which we stand" by faith (Rom. 5:2) now "[trains] us to renounce ungodliness and worldly passions, and to live self-controlled, upright, and godly lives in the present age" as we await the return of "our great God and Savior Jesus Christ" (Titus 2:12–13).

We who "have died to the law through the body of Christ" now "belong to another, to him who has been raised from the dead, *in order that* we may bear fruit for God" rather than "fruit for death" (Rom. 7:4-5, emphasis added). We were "created in Christ Jesus *for* good works, which God prepared beforehand, that we should walk in them" (Eph. 2:10, emphasis added). Therefore, even though our good works contribute absolutely nothing to our salvation (see Eph. 2:9), they are clearly part of the purpose for which God saved us "by grace" and "made us alive together with Christ" (Eph. 2:5). Indeed, "we were buried . . . with [Christ] by baptism into death, *in order that*, just as Christ was raised from the dead by the glory of the Father, we too might walk in *newness* of life" (Rom. 6:4, emphasis added).

"You are not your own," Paul writes elsewhere to the Corinthians, "for you were bought with a price" (1 Cor. 6:19–20, 7:23). You were redeemed from your slavery to sin and death by nothing less than the blood of Christ (see Eph. 1:7). Therefore, "we are debtors, not to the flesh, to live according to the flesh" (Rom. 8:12), but to Christ—to live according to *his* will by *his* Spirit. For Christ "died for all, that those who live might no longer live for themselves but for him who for their sake died and was raised" (2 Cor. 5:15). He "gave himself for us" not only to save us from God's wrath to come but also "to redeem us from all lawlessness and to purify for himself a people *for his own possession* who are zealous *for good works*" (Titus 2:14, emphasis added). So, in response to the one who set us free from the bondage of sin, we should daily count ourselves free as we endeavor to walk in those good works for his glory.

Commanded to Do Good

The command to love one another also isn't telling us to simply sit around and wait for such love to arise before we do anything. Such impractical wisdom ultimately represents a misleading way of restating the reality that we simply don't love one another as we should. The same is also true of the seemingly opposite notion that we should somehow "fake it 'til we make it." If, indeed, people have to fake a love for their neighbor, then they, by definition, don't love their neighbor. Therefore, they are breaking the command to love their neighbor as themselves. And that's a sin.

Nevertheless, "as we have opportunity" to do so (Gal. 6:10), we should "always seek to do good to one another and to everyone" (1 Thess. 5:15) regardless of how we feel. Having been saved "according to [God's] own mercy" and "justified by his grace," we must "be careful to devote [ourselves] to good works" (Titus 3:5–8). Even if we don't genuinely love our enemies, for example, we are not thereby exempted from the Lord's separate command to do good to them (see Luke 6:27; Rom. 12:20). However, the specific command to *love* them *also* still remains.

C. S. Lewis, who is incalculably more intelligent than I, once wrote the following in his famous book *Mere Christianity*:

> The rule for all of us is perfectly simple. Do not waste time bothering whether you "love" your neighbour; act as if you did. As soon as we do this we find one of the great secrets. When you are behaving as if you loved someone, you will presently come to love him.[2]

I cannot as confidently agree that this secret always proves true. Nor can I cite any promise in the Bible that guarantees that if we will just act as if we love someone, the emotion will eventually follow. Perhaps the emotion *won't* follow much of the time, but Lewis prudently points out that often it will. Indeed, because of the cultivating influence they have on our values and beliefs, the decisions we make and the actions we take can profoundly impact what we come to love. Nevertheless, even if a genuine love *does* follow such intentional action, as Lewis suggests, it must still be understood as the direct result of the Holy Spirit's work within us.

So you can certainly "act" as if you loved others in the sense that you can do good to them even when you

---

2. C.S. Lewis, *Mere Christianity* (New York: Simon & Schuster, 1996), 116.

feel no love for them. In fact, you *should* do that. You should do to others "whatever you wish that others would do to you" (Matt. 7:12) regardless of how you feel about them. But you should also genuinely love those people. And for such genuine love to arise within us, we remain dependent on the Spirit. As we seek to renew our minds, he alone can take us from *acting* as if we love someone to *actually* loving that someone just as Christ loved us.

I understand that this connection between emotion and sin may be difficult to digest. However, we must not attempt to bypass this offensive conclusion by mistakenly blaming our lack of emotion on *love's* nature rather than on our own *sinful* nature. Otherwise, we would miss this opportunity for God's perfect standard to absolutely crush any last hope we might have in our own ability to fulfill it apart from Christ. In other words, when we understand that God's standard demands even our emotions to fall in line, our sinfulness is exposed beyond measure. We see even more clearly that "none is righteous, no, not one" (Rom. 3:10). We become even more thankful that God "saved us, not because of works done by *us* in righteousness, but according to *his* own mercy" (Titus 3:5, emphasis added). And we draw even more comfort from knowing we "are justified by his grace as a gift, through the redemption that is in Christ Jesus" (Rom. 3:24).

Our hope and confidence in the midst of our fluctu-ating emotions does not rest in some novel definition of love that makes our sin seem a little less severe. No, our hope and confidence rests in Christ and his unfluctuating gospel of grace, for he redeemed us from our sin so severe when he "gave himself as a ransom for all" (1 Tim. 2:6).

Chapter 12

A CAREFUL DISTINCTION

To be clear, C. S. Lewis would most certainly not agree that love is an emotion. Shortly before his statement referenced previously, he writes:

> But love, in the Christian sense, does not mean an emotion. It is a state not of the feelings but of the will; that state of the will which we have naturally about ourselves, and must learn to have about other people.[1]

A couple of pages later, he likewise writes, "Christian Love, either towards God or towards man, is an affair of the will."[2]

---

1. Lewis, *Mere Christianity*, 115.
2. Lewis, 117–118.

Insomuch as an affair of the will is some kind of action or decision or commitment, I obviously cannot agree with Lewis's definition of love based on the arguments I've already presented. Much of what Lewis writes in both *Mere Christianity* and *The Four Loves* rests on the misguided understanding that *agapē* love is some kind of selfless love uniquely exercised by the believer. He seems to equate loving someone with behaving as *if* you loved that someone. But doesn't the very notion of behaving as *if* you loved someone imply you actually *don't* love that someone?

Nevertheless, even though Lewis and I disagree about love's being an emotion, I agree with the overall sentiment of his previously cited "rule for all." His aim, after all, is practical. Rather than analyzing our emotions to the point of self-absorbed paralysis, Lewis wants us to take hold of the freedom we have in Christ to *do* something. To those who "are told they ought to love God" but "cannot find any such feeling in themselves," Lewis offers the following solution: "Do not sit trying to manufacture feelings. Ask yourself, 'If I were sure that I loved God, what would I do?' When you have found the answer, go and do it."[3]

_____

3. Lewis, 117.

To me, Lewis's advice is not altogether unlike Paul's previously mentioned admonition to make use of every opportunity God gives us to "do good to everyone" (Gal. 6:10). The specific focus in both cases rests not on how we should feel about those around us but on our obligation to do good to those around us regardless of how we may feel about them. And that's an important command to heed. Yet as I read Lewis's work, I struggle to find any clear distinction between his concept of loving someone and the biblical concept of doing good to that someone. Without that distinction in place, the implied imperative then becomes that we should love our neighbors as ourselves *by* doing good to them. However, God clearly commands us both to love our neighbors as ourselves *and* to do good to them. Despite the intimate interplay that may exist between these two commands, they *are*, in fact, distinct.

Even though Lewis's advice may prove helpful from a practical standpoint, I would add at least one preliminary step that would likely be deemed unnecessary from his point of view. Whenever you don't feel much love for God or your neighbor, humbly acknowledge your lack of love and recognize it for the sin it is. Let it then prompt a moment of thanksgiving for the one who freely died for that sin on the cross—the one in whom you, by God's grace alone, have been forgiven, justified, adopted, redeemed, and renewed. Amen!

After that, in the words of Lewis, "do not waste time bothering whether you 'love' your neighbor"[4] whenever the opportunity arises for you to do good to him or her. Instead, understand that you are free to take that opportunity "to the glory of God" (1 Cor. 10:31). And all along the way, ask God to produce a great love within you because you are powerless to produce such love on your own.

Pursuing Love

We aren't supposed to passively wait around for love to arise within us before we do any good works. On the contrary, Paul repeatedly admonishes us to *pursue . . . love* as we "fight the good fight of the faith" (1 Tim. 6:11–12, emphasis added; see also 1 Cor. 14:1; 2 Tim. 2:22). Surely, this intentional pursuit of love includes a disciplined determination to do the very things that such love will always do (i.e., such love will always fulfill God's commands). Surely, it also includes an unrelenting resolution to avoid the very things such love will never do (i.e., such love will always avoid sin). But ultimately, above all else, it requires us to continually look to Christ as we view his commands through the lens of his gospel. We must frame every instruction he gives us within the context of what he already did for us on the cross. Otherwise, we will fail to discern just how vast a difference lies between living "under law" and living "under grace" through faith (Rom. 6:14).

---

4. Lewis, 116.

For example, while the law *requires* obedience in order for those under it to *gain* righteousness and life, God's grace *incites* obedience by proclaiming that, in Christ, we already *have* righteousness and life. It beckons us to "walk in love" for one another by pointing to the way in which Christ first loved us (Eph. 5:2). It compels us to forgive one another by reminding us that "God in Christ forgave [us]" (Eph. 4:32).[5] It urges us to "walk as children of light" by explaining that we already "are light in the Lord" (Eph. 5:8). And only *after* teaching us that we are adopted children of God (see Eph. 1:5) who have an inheritance in Christ (see Eph. 1:11) guaranteed by the Spirit within us (see Eph. 1:14) does God's grace then train us *not* to live like "the sons of disobedience" who have no such inheritance (Eph. 5:6). Only after declaring that we "have been raised with Christ" (Col. 3:1) does it then bid us to "put to death . . . what is earthly in [us]" as a result (Col. 3:5).

In short, the gospel of the grace of God invites us to learn of all its glorious implications and daily reckon those truths to be so. It beseeches us to "put off [our] old self" (Eph. 4:22) because that is no longer who we are. It entreats us to "put on the new self" instead (Eph. 4:24)

---

5. Contrast this understanding of forgiveness with the conditional statement Jesus makes to those who are under the law: "If you forgive others their trespasses, your heavenly Father will also forgive you, but if you do not forgive others their trespasses, neither will your Father forgive your trespasses" (Matt. 6:14–15).

because that is actually who we are in Christ. And for us to be able to do those two things—for us to be able to walk according to who we already are—we need "to be renewed in the spirit of [our] minds" (Eph. 4:23) through our increasing knowledge of the one who recreated us (see Col. 3:10).

Therefore, while I don't think we should ignore or deny our lack of love whenever we notice it, I also don't think we should spend too much time focusing on it. Instead, after we identify it as sin, we should focus on the one who has saved us from that sin by grace through faith. And we should do this knowing that our faith in him and what he has done for us will only end up motivating the love we have for both him and one another.

This shift of focus must not be confused, however, with a flippant attitude toward sin. No, our sin remains the wretched and reprehensible thing for which Christ had to die to save us. But therein lies the point. Christ *did* die for our sins. Hence, when we respond to our sin by focusing on him, we allow for at least two important things to occur.

First, we let his gospel comfort our hearts by reminding us we can unashamedly trust in his sufficient sacrifice on our behalf—even when we are grieved, for instance, by the sin we just committed moments ago. We can humbly yet boldly proclaim that in Christ we stand forgiven and justified by his blood. Second, we let it reshape our perspective by reminding us that "our old self was crucified *with* him" on that cross "so that we would no longer be enslaved to sin" (Rom. 6:6, emphasis added). Consequently, by recalling that we are now "dead to sin and alive to God in Christ Jesus" (Rom. 6:11), we grow more eager to honor and serve him "as those who have been brought from death to life" (Rom. 6:13). And rather than view his gospel as something we believe only to *begin* our Christian lives, we start to view it as the bountiful wellspring from which we will draw strength for the *rest* of our lives.

Of course, many people insist we can also choose love whenever we don't feel love by purposefully setting our minds on and directing our actions toward the things that help cultivate such love. And that's great advice. However, because love is an emotion that we cannot simply decide to genuinely feel, whenever we claim to be "choosing" love, I contend we are technically choosing, rather, to *pursue* love. And as I referenced at the beginning of this section, that is exactly what Paul encourages us to do. So, insomuch as choosing love can be more accurately understood as pursuing love, let's continue to do so fervently. Ultimately, I have no desire to quarrel over a verbal cue that has proved so helpful for so many.

Chapter 13

LOOKING OUTSIDE OURSELVES

P aul tells the Corinthians, "Let all that you do be done in love" (1 Cor. 16:14). In other words, let every act you ever do be done out of a love you can genuinely feel. Of course, Paul is not referring to just any kind of love. No, he is referring to the perfect love with which Christ first loved us. Such love carries not even an ounce of selfish ambition and thus naturally fulfills every command given to believers in the body of Christ. Such love also conforms to the widely cherished description Paul eloquently provides a few chapters earlier in that same letter.

Love is patient and kind; love does not envy or boast; it is not arrogant or rude. It does not insist on its own way; it is not irritable or resentful; it does not rejoice at wrongdoing, but rejoices with the truth. Love bears all things, believes all things, hopes all things, endures all things.

—1 Cor. 13:4–7

Who except Christ could ever successfully walk in such perfect love? Certainly not me.

Honestly, I don't know if I've ever done one thing out of nothing but pure love for my neighbor. Even if I have—which I seriously doubt—I still have no way of confirming I have because only God can see the true intentions hidden within our hearts (see Ps. 19:12; Prov. 16:2; 1 Cor. 4:3–5; 1 Thess. 2:4). Despite whatever love we may feel for one another, we can never be fully certain our motivation is not at least partially selfish. And thanks to the sinful flesh that unfortunately still lingers within us, our motivation probably *is* at least partially selfish.

For this reason, among many, the notion that love is an emotion can be a truly frightening one to accept. At least it most certainly was for me. It made me realize my sinful condition apart from Christ was far worse than I could ever imagine. It also handed me a stinging dose of humility and conviction that left me doubting whether God could truly be merciful to such a wretched sinner like me.

Yet who did God send his Son into this world to save? According to the apostle Paul, who "formerly . . . was a blasphemer, persecutor, and insolent opponent" (1 Tim. 1:13), the answer is certain.

> *The saying is trustworthy and deserving of full acceptance, that Christ Jesus came into the world to save* sinners, *of whom I am the foremost. But I received mercy for this reason, that in me, as the foremost, Jesus Christ might display his perfect patience as an example to those who were to believe in him for eternal life* (emphasis added).
>
> —1 Tim. 1:15–16

Clearly, Christ came into the world to save sinners like you and me. And clearly, the grace that first overflowed for Paul (see 1 Tim. 1:14) now overflows for all who believe in the gospel he was taught by the ascended Lord to preach. So, while the understanding that love is an emotion may painfully add to the "knowledge of [our] sin" (Rom. 3:20), that conviction is meant to lead us to *Christ*, "in whom we have redemption, the forgiveness of [our] sins" (Col. 1:14). It is meant to lead us to the gospel of God's grace that then turns our sorrow into thanksgiving and praise.

But what if it doesn't?

What if this deeper understanding of our sin does nothing but discourage us? Worse yet, what if it causes us to question whether we have honestly even been saved?

How should we respond to whatever doubt or distress may arise?

As I have sought to clarify throughout this book, salvation is a free gift from God that comes by grace through faith in the person and work of Jesus Christ—not through any love or good works of our own (see Eph. 2:8–9). Consequently, absolutely no amount of love or good works on our part can ever confirm or deny our salvation because such love and good works never served as the basis for our salvation.

So if you ever find yourself doubting whether you have been saved by God, don't go looking to your moral performance or past experiences for some kind of assurance, confidence, or esoteric indicator of spiritual status. Don't even go looking to whatever faith you think you have lest you become the victim of your own subjective and ultimately misguided introspection. Instead, in response to your feelings of uncertainty, you must look outside yourself to the object of your faith—"Jesus Christ and him crucified" *for you* and *for your sin* (1 Cor. 2:2). All other ground for assurance will prove to be nothing but sinking sand.

The sure and *sole* proof of our salvation resides not in ourselves but in the historical fact "that Christ died for our sins in accordance with the Scriptures," was "buried," and "was raised on the third day in accordance with the Scriptures" (1 Cor. 15:3–4). He then appeared to hundreds of witnesses (see 1 Cor. 15:5–8), many of whom willingly died for the sake of their testimony of him. Yes, Christ "was delivered up for our trespasses and raised for our justification" (Rom. 4:25) so God could freely and justly save sinners "to the praise of his glorious grace" (Eph. 1:6). While this "word of the cross" may be "folly to those who are perishing" (1 Cor. 1:18), it "is the power of God for salvation to everyone who believes" (Rom. 1:16).

Therefore, if you have heard and believed in this great "gospel of your salvation" (Eph. 1:13), you can be objectively assured that God has saved you on the basis of Christ and his finished work alone. You have been saved "by grace . . . through faith" apart from any doing of your own (Eph. 2:8). For "to the one who does not work but believes in him who justifies the ungodly, his faith is counted as righteousness" (Rom. 4:5), and he has "peace with God through our Lord Jesus Christ" (Rom. 5:1). He has been qualified by the Father "to share in the inheritance of the saints in light" (Col. 1:12). And he has been "delivered . . . from the domain of darkness and transferred . . . to the kingdom of [God's] beloved Son" (Col. 1:13).

As we ponder this great salvation and revel in "the immeasurable riches of [God's] grace in kindness toward us in Christ Jesus" (Eph. 2:7), may we always remember God saved us "because of the great love with which *he* loved *us*" first (Eph. 2:4, emphasis added)—not the other way around. Indeed, our love is only a response to his love—a love so deep and vast that it truly "surpasses knowledge" (Eph. 3:19). And as we forever seek to comprehend this love from which nothing "in all creation" will ever "be able to separate us" (Rom. 8:38–39), may we find joy in the confident conviction that God actually *feels* it—and infinitely so.

ACKNOWLEDGMENTS

I would like to thank my wife, Kayla, for being the kind of woman who makes me want to shout "I love this girl" from the rooftops. There is an embarrassingly long list of things I honestly couldn't do without her, and finishing this project is certainly one of them. While I may have written a tiny book about selfless love, she's the one who actually shows that kind of love so beautifully on a daily basis. I still find it hard to believe that I get to be married to someone so far out of my league.

I would like to thank my mom for the tears I know she's going to shed when she reads this part. They are tears produced by a heart that has been through so much but has come out so strong. She's a joy and inspiration to anyone who ever meets her. And she's more excited about this book than I am. That makes me smile.

I would like to thank my brother for being the kind of man a younger sibling would be proud to emulate. If I have any measure of passion for the Lord, it's because I first saw my brother with 10 times more. I don't think I'll ever be able to catch up to him in that regard. That's okay, though. I'll just keep looking up to him.

I would also like to thank my brother's beautiful wife for somehow finding it in her heart to put up with the guy (he is still my brother after all).

I would like to thank my dad for encouraging me to pursue something I love and for working so hard to make that pursuit possible.

I would like to thank Ken for the inspiration and support I know he would have lavished upon me if he had only been given the chance.

I would like to thank Dr. Matthew A. Elliott, although I have never met him, for being crazy enough to believe that love is an emotion long before I did.

I would like to thank Linda Stubbefield for being the first editor to take a stab at this manuscript and for indirectly trying to teach me the difference between writing for myself and writing for others. I would also like to thank the entire staff at Lucid Books for being an absolute joy to work with throughout the publishing process.

I would like to thank all the local coffee shops in Houston, Texas, especially Boomtown, EQ Heights, A Second Cup, and Black Hole. I would also like to thank all the other regulars there who unknowingly became my coworkers.

Finally, I would like to thank a handful of my dear friends. Despite my unfortunate habit of unexpectedly going underground at times, they graciously choose to stick around as loving examples in my life.

Mike Reese for being a rock and a legend and for letting me crash on his couch way longer than he probably should have.

Nate Russ for being the passionate adventurer I hope to be like when I grow up and for braving my most "sick and tired" days while riding his scooter in the freezing rain.

Andrew Robertson for being my closest friend no matter how much time has passed and for always being up for an ice cream run even if he has to sit in the back seat.

Michael Frnka for being one of the most genuine guys anyone could ever meet and for forgiving me after I accidentally spit water on his Bible.

Donivan Brown for being the kind of friend and influence that words simply cannot describe and for indubitably earning the title of most interesting man alive.

CPSIA information can be obtained
at www.ICGtesting.com
Printed in the USA
LVHW011147160521
687570LV00010B/182